MW00464270

the STORY of MOM

A QUESTION & ANSWER GUIDE TO

Mom's Life, Lessons, and Legacy

VANESSA PARKS

ADAMS MEDIA
New York London Toronto Sydney New Delhi

Adams Media
An Imprint of Simon & Schuster, Inc.
57 Littlefield Street
Avon, Massachusetts 02322

First Adams Media hardcover edition April 2021

ADAMS MEDIA and colophon are trademarks of Simon & Schuster.

For information about special discounts for bulk purchases, please contact Simon & Schuster Special Sales at 1-866-506-1949 or business@simonandschuster.com.

The Simon & Schuster Speakers Bureau can bring authors to your live event. For more information or to book an event contact the Simon & Schuster Speakers Bureau at 1-866-248-3049 or visit our website at www.simonspeakers.com.

Interior design by Priscilla Yuen
Interior images © 123RF/annaguz

Manufactured in China

10 9 8 7 6 5 4 3 2 1

Library of Congress Cataloging-in-Publication Data has been applied for.

ISBN 978-1-5072-1554-8

ACKNOWLEDGMENTS

Thanks a bunch to everyone who offered thoughts on what they'd like to know about their own moms, especially my nieces, Kelly Breiner (mother of Abigail and Luke/daughter of Patty) and Alison Amorello Seibold (mother of J.D./daughter of Mary). It's been so fun watching them become the wonderful mothers they are.

Thanks also to friends who went above and beyond with their thoughts: Janet Amorello (mother of Sam/ daughter of Louise), Kathi Scrizzi Driscoll (mother of Molly and Meg/daughter of Millie), Mary Grauerholz (mother of Ben and Charro/daughter of Ruth), and Linda Harrington (mother of Lauren, Lindsay, Robert, and Kevin/daughter of Kathy).

And to my daughter, Tess, who is smart, funny, and kind.

CONTENTS

INTRODUCTION

Hey, Mom...

If you could travel anywhere tomorrow, where would you go?

What was the first thing you learned to cook?

What do you remember most about the place where you grew up?

What are you most proud of in your life?

If you could pick a day to relive, what would it be?

Your mom has been around your whole life, but how much do you really know about this special woman? There's probably a good chance that your conversations with Mom have fallen into a familiar, uninspired pattern: what happened at work, what's going on with the kids, how other family members are doing, maybe even the weather.

Yet there's so much more to learn! And if you don't ask, you'll never know!

That's where *The Story of Mom: A Question & Answer Guide to Mom's Life, Lessons, and Legacy* comes in. The more than one hundred questions you'll find inside cover a variety of topics: her early years, her work life, parenting, relationships, likes and dislikes, pivotal moments, amusing anecdotes, perhaps a tragic tale or two. In short, the stuff of which family stories are made. These stories will entertain you, ground you, nurture your relationship with your mom, and remind you of where and how you fit in and belong.

The insights you glean from these questions may be among the best gifts you and your family ever receive. While an heirloom like a wedding ring or painting can be enjoyed by just one person—though perhaps coveted by many—family stories can be enjoyed and owned by all. Here's to *The Story of Mom*, a treasure to be passed on for generations.

HOW TO USE THIS BOOK

This book was envisioned to be a conversation between you and your mom (or stepmom or grandmother). Though you can give Mom the book and have her answer the questions, a better plan is to sit with her and channel your inner Oprah. Interview her—and know that the best, fullest answers will come from follow-up questions.

The first chapter contains easy, basic questions about family background and favorite things, making it a great ice-breaker. Rather than run through all these questions at once, you may want to save a few for each sitting. And, no, you won't get through all the questions in one sitting. It will take time.

Plan to meet when you'll both be relaxed and not rushed, in a comfortable place where you won't be interrupted but will be able to take breaks. Then plan to meet again. And maybe again. Perhaps siblings will want to share the experience of compiling *The Story of Mom*, taking turns at chapters.

There's space on the pages for written answers, which can be filled by either you or Mom. You may want to bring your computer or a recording app—or both—to capture Mom's responses, so you don't miss a moment. Keep in mind that you'll have to transcribe the recording later. (At the beginning of the recording, you may want to state the date and who's speaking. Try to eliminate any background noise.)

Some questions are meant to elicit longer answers than others. The follow-up questions that are provided will be essential for drawing out a full story. If Mom seems stuck on a question, you might rephrase it so it isn't a superlative. For instance, if she can't quite come up with the worst this or the best that, ask her to think of "one of the best" or "one of the worst." Or you might coax an answer by offering what your answer might be.

But don't rush to fill a void of silence. Be patient. It will give Mom time to ponder. Or perhaps prompt her to fill the silence! But if an answer isn't coming, move on. Come back to a question that requires ruminating...but remember to come back to it—a third or fourth time, if necessary.

End each session with a tentative time for the next one.

You'll also find space to include photos of your mom and some other important family shots. Try to include at least one photograph from all phases of Mom's life: a baby picture, photos of her as a young child and teenager, school photos, a graduation photo, maybe a wedding photo. These photos will add a visual element to this record of your mom's life.

When *The Story of Mom* is complete, be sure to share it with younger family members. It will help them build an identity, construct their own story, and feel even more connected to the people they love.

CHAPTER 1

Quick Questions about Mom's Background and Favorite Things

Consider this opening chapter an icebreaker, with short-answer questions about Mom's background and favorite things. These questions should be easy to answer, which is why we suggest not running through all of them at once. Instead, start off each session with a few of these questions before delving into questions in later chapters that will require more thought.

You may know the answers to some of these questions already, but we're betting you don't know all of them. Or maybe you think you know the answer and will be surprised to discover that you're wrong. Her favorite color? Easy. Her favorite sound? Maybe not.

Whether or not you know the answers, it's worthwhile to have them recorded for future generations. Perhaps someday a granddaughter or great-grandson will delight in discovering that Grandma's or Great-Grandma's favorite food was pasta or ice cream—just like them! Or perhaps they'll hear a song in the coming years and, knowing it was her favorite song, remember Grandma with a smile. What could be sweeter than that?

Where and when were you born?

Name your siblings from oldest to youngest. Where were you in the birth order?

Let's construct your family tree. Name your parents, grandparents, and great-grandparents, and, if you know them, the dates they were born and died.

What's your ethnic background?

Where did you go to school (elementary, high school, undergrad, postgrad, other)?

What are your children's names? Grandchildren?

What's your favorite movie and who's your favorite actor?

What's your favorite food?

What's your favorite song? What's your pump-up song?

Tell me your favorite color.

Your favorite animal?

What was your best birthday?

What's a sound that you love?

CHAPTER 2

Once Upon a Time: Mom's Childhood

Your vision of who Mom was as a child and teen probably consists of images in old photographs. Unless you've heard her reminisce with her siblings or old friends, you may not realize that Mom was, say, painfully shy. Or maybe a bit of a wild child.

The questions in this chapter touch upon things like where Mom grew up, her friends, and how she enjoyed spending time as a child. It's always fun to hear childhood stories about someone you've only ever known as an adult. And while you may have heard these stories about your partner or spouse, for some reason, we don't always get the chance to hear stories that reveal who Mom was as a little girl and teen.

These Once Upon a Time questions also explore her relationships with her parents, siblings, and other meaningful people in her life. Will it surprise you to learn that Uncle Ned was her favorite sibling? Other questions in this chapter will delve a little deeper. Take a closer look at what Mom's childhood was like. Discover the experiences that helped shape the woman she is today. Take that faded photograph and watch it develop into a fuller picture of just who Mom was, and is.

What do you remember most about the place where you grew up?
What feelings does it evoke when you recall it?

What was your favorite childhood game or way to spend time?

Who was your best friend as a child? What's one word he or she might use to describe you as a kid? When was the last time you were in touch?

How would you describe your parents? Did you get along well with them? How did this evolve as you got older? Were you closer to your mother or your father?

Can you share a family story that your family used to tell when you were young? Did you ask them to tell it or would they bring it up on their own? What did you enjoy about this piece of family lore? What did you learn from it?

Did you have a happy childhood? Why or why not? What would you change about it today, if you could? Did this influence how you raised us?

What kind of child were you—well behaved or rebellious? What about each of your siblings? Who among you was the most obedient, and who was the least?

What was your relationship with your siblings like? Who was your favorite? Is he/she still your favorite today? What changed?

Who was your favorite relative growing up? Why?

What did you want to be when you were growing up?

What year of adolescence did you most enjoy? Least enjoy?

Would you say you were confident or awkward? What were your insecurities? Did you eventually get over them? When? What helped you get over them, or prevented you from doing so?

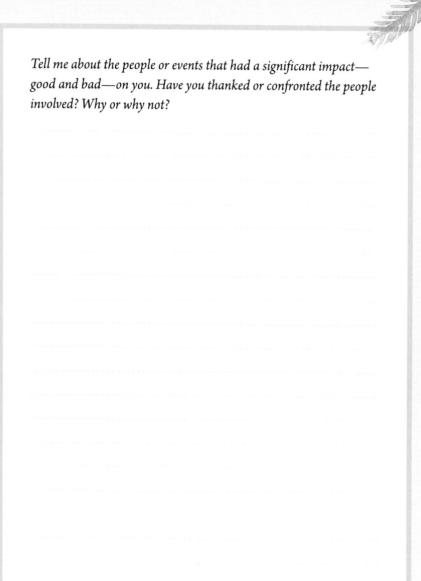

Tell me about the people or events that had a significant impact—good and bad—on you. Have you thanked or confronted the people involved? Why or why not?

CHAPTER 3

Romance and Other Novel Experiences

As Mom moved into her teen years and beyond, she no doubt discovered a world of new experiences, like love and independence. Is Mom a hopeless romantic or the strong and steady type? What are her thoughts on love and love at first sight? Has she been unlucky in love?

While Mom and Dad, or Mom and Mom, may have been a couple all your life, it wasn't always thus. What came before? And what about the two of them? What was her first impression of him or her?

It may be hard to imagine Mom as a flirtatious young belle or as a giddy lovesick girl. But pursuing love and being in love is yet another dimension of her personality. If this isn't the kind of thing Mom typically opens up about, here's your chance to pry without feeling like you're prying.

This chapter focuses largely on love and romance, but of course those aren't the only novel experiences for a young person transitioning from adolescence to adulthood. There's also moving out of the home where she grew up, a first car, learning to cook, having a drink. Let's pull back the curtain and take a peek.

How old were you when you had your first kiss? Did you do it out of curiosity or desire? Who was it with? Was there a second kiss?

Do you believe in love at first sight?

Tell me about your first serious relationship. How old were you?
How did it end? Do you ever think about him or her?

What was the craziest thing you did with your girlfriends in high school? Would you do it again if you could? Did you all talk about it much as the years went by?

What was the make and color of your first car? How did you acquire it?

How old were you when you moved out of your parents' home?
Where did you move? What cities have you lived in?

Did your spouse or partner have a pet name for you? Did you have one for them?

Do you remember the first time you saw your husband/wife/partner and what your impression was? How did you meet? What about your husband/wife/partner attracted you to him/her? How long did you date? What was the proposal like? How long were you engaged before you got married or moved in together?

What was the first thing you learned to cook?

Do you remember the first time you got a little tipsy? How about a time you definitely got too tipsy? Tell me how old you were, whom you were with, and where you were.

Tell me about something adventurous you've done. Were you nervous or excited or both? Did you ever do it again? Would you like to do it again?

Would you share a toothbrush with your partner?

Have you kept any secrets from your spouse/partner? Care to share them, or at least tell me what they involved generally, without getting into specifics? Why didn't you want your spouse to know about this? Do you regret keeping the secrets, or do you consider them either harmless or better left unknown?

Tell me about a time that you had your heart broken. How long did it take to get over it? Do you ever think about that person? Did you break someone else's heart? What about other types of heartbreak?

What's the most romantic moment you've experienced?

CHAPTER 4

Character Development: What Makes Mom Mom

They say that adversity builds character, but almost all other life experiences do as well. Someone's character is the totality of qualities that define them. The questions here will explore Mom's psyche, perceptions, and moral qualities.

We're betting that many of the questions in this chapter aren't ones that you've ever asked Mom, or that you know the answer to. And they may not be questions that Mom has actively contemplated. This, then, may be one of those chapters that takes more time and requires you to remember those interviewing techniques in the How to Use This Book section. (Try to be comfortable with silence while Mom contemplates an answer. Maybe you can prompt a response by suggesting what your answer might be. And recognize when it's time to move on, but be sure to revisit the question in a subsequent session.)

What is your mom's greatest fear? What is she most proud of? Do any of her personality traits make her cringe? What makes her most content? The responses to these questions will offer a glimpse into Mom's internal world and deepen your understanding of what makes Mom Mom.

What age do you feel you are (that is, your subjective age versus your actual age)? Has this always been the age you've felt you are, more or less?

What are you most proud of in your life, and why? What's something you're not so proud of, and why? Have the types of things that make you proud changed as you've gone through life?

Which of your senses would you most hate to lose: Sight or hearing? Taste or smell or touch?

Have you cried recently? Why? What about a good laugh?

What personality trait do you have that doesn't make you happy?
Do you try to work on it? Where do you think it comes from? How
do you feel when you see it come out? Now tell me about a fine trait
of yours.

What is your greatest fear? Have you ever had to face it? Do you have any lesser fears or phobias, like a fear of public speaking or a fear of snakes?

Complete this sentence:
I believe that people are basically _____
_____ *. Why do you feel this way?*

In what moments are you most content? What about these moments gives you that sense of inner peace? Do you experience them often enough? Do you seek them out?

How do you pull yourself out of a bad mood?

Tell me something about yourself that would surprise me, or that no one knows. Do you intentionally not talk about this, or has it just never come up?

Are you a trusting or distrustful person? What events in your life have helped foster this? Do you wish that you were more trusting or less so?

Imagine you were in a difficult situation, like stranded on an island or taken hostage. What qualities would you rely upon to survive?

Is there an old wives' tale or expression, such as "You can't have your cake and eat it too," that you've never quite understood or agreed with?

What's the most challenging mental or physical health issue with which you've had to deal? At what point in your life did you have to deal with this? What was challenging about it? Would you deal with it differently today?

CHAPTER 5

The Plot Thickens: Pregnancy, Motherhood, and Family Life

Long before she was your mom, she was her mother's daughter. That relationship most surely influenced her relationship with you. Which is why this chapter explores not just Mom's thoughts on being a mother but also what her relationship was like with her own parents and family. Did your mom want to be the same kind of mother her own mother was? In what ways?

Eventually she became a mother, an experience that manages to be both magical and challenging. What most surprised your mom about becoming a mother? Did she enjoy being pregnant?

As you and your siblings were growing up, there most likely were countless times when you said or did something so adorable that it melted Mom's heart. Surely Mom has some favorite moments as a parent that she can share with you—as well as those moments that were the worst.

And finally, if she hadn't been a mom, how would her life be different? It's time to find out.

Did you enjoy being pregnant or not so much? How did your deliveries go with each of us? How long were you in labor? Were you calm or a screamer?

For adoptive moms: Tell me about the day you first met me.

How did you choose the names that you gave each of us?

What most surprised you about becoming a mother? Did you expect something else or had you not given it any thought beforehand?

In what stage of a child's life is parenting easiest? What stage is hardest?

Is there anything you did as a mother that's unacceptable by today's standards, like driving without a car seat? Was there something advocated by parenting books that you embraced but now consider hogwash?

Did you want to be the same kind of mother that your mother was?
In what ways? What did you want to do differently?

What was one of your favorite moments as a parent? What was one of the worst? How did each make you feel?

Was there a moment when you questioned your parenting judgment? How did that affect you?

Do you wish you had disciplined us differently? Did you read a lot of parenting books?

What's your favorite family tradition? Why?

What would you change about your family dynamic growing up, and with our family dynamic?

If you hadn't had children, how would your life be different? Would you have more children or fewer children if you could go back in time?

What's a piece of advice you would offer a new mom?

CHAPTER 6

Judge a Book by Its Cover: Fun and Frivolous Musings

Admit it, you've judged a book by its cover at one point or another. And sometimes, superficial is fun. We suspect that going through the questions in this chapter will be entertaining. They're the kinds of things you might know had you been a dear friend of Mom's for many years.

You may be thinking, "Well, Mom and I are good friends." But it's important to note that mothers and their children are not peers. A generation ago, relationships between mothers and daughters eventually evolved into a kind of friendship, but there remained a clear distinction between the two. Mothers and daughters today are far more likely to discuss intimate matters and consider each other good friends.

So here you will learn some things her peers may know already, like the most repulsive thing she's ever eaten, or what celebrity she'd most like to date. You may also find out that Mom, like most women, can be critical of her own appearance, and what she would change about her looks if she could.

The questions in this chapter will reveal Mom's feelings about things like her own looks, aging, and fashion.

What do you consider your best physical feature? Did you always feel this way? Is there anything you wish you could change about your appearance? Have you changed anything about your appearance? Are you more or less critical of your looks now, as compared with when you were younger?

What was your worst look in terms of fashion? What about your worst hairstyle or makeup choice? How long did you embrace it? How old were you?

What's a favorite piece of clothing that you've owned? How did you feel wearing it? What about favorite shoes?

What was your worst beauty experience (for example, a burnt upper lip from waxing, a horrible haircut, or an outfit that wasn't appropriate for the occasion)?

When did you start coloring your hair, and why?

What's the most repulsive thing you've ever drank or eaten? Tell me about the circumstances.

Do you remember the first time that something made you feel old, like noticing how young a police officer or physician looked? What makes you feel old now? Do you mind feeling old or do you embrace it?

How do you feel about getting older... the good, the bad, and the ugly? What makes you feel young? Which is preferable, being old or being young? Why?

Do you consider yourself athletic? What is your favorite sport to watch or participate in? What do you do for exercise?

What's something sentimental that you bought for yourself and when did you buy it? Did you have to talk yourself into it or was it an impulse? Do you still own it? If so, does it give you a bit of joy?

If you could go on a date with any celebrity (assume both of you are single), who would it be? What would you like to do?

What are your thoughts on astrology? What's your zodiac sign?

Tell me about a time that you judged a book by its cover and were completely wrong. Do you think it's sometimes possible to accurately judge someone by their looks? Do you think we as a society put too much stock in appearances?

If you had to choose between movies, music, or books for the rest of your life, what would you go with, and why?

CHAPTER 7

Textbook Lessons from School, Work, and Life

Most people usually view their mothers as, well, mothers. Can you remember the last time you got a glimpse of her as a person separate from her maternal role? She spent years as a student and working before she became a parent, and perhaps after. Who is she when she isn't with you?

Take, for example, those years as a student. Did she like school? Was she an average student? What about favorite subjects? And her work life. If statistics bear out, she may have grappled with some of the same issues that are finally being addressed with the Time's Up movement. Was she ever undervalued because she was a woman?

If she could embark on an entirely different career, what would it be? Is there something new she'd like to learn? What's holding her back? (A gift certificate to pursue this interest could be your next present to her!) Does her greatest accomplishment have something to do with work, or learning, or being a mother? Or none of these?

In this chapter you'll learn about various aspects of Mom's life, including her time at school, working outside the home, and as a student of life.

Did you enjoy school? Why or why not? What kind of student were you? What was your favorite subject? Did you speak up in class? Who was your favorite teacher and why? What did you usually have for lunch?

What's something you've always wanted to learn to do but didn't? (Maybe something like learning another language, playing an instrument, or baking the perfect chocolate soufflé.) Why didn't you learn? Would you consider doing it now?

If you had been born at a later time or could choose another career, what do you see yourself doing? Why?

What was your first job, and how old were you? Did you enjoy it? What was your favorite job? Why? What did you learn from your least favorite job?

Share with me an important lesson you've learned in life. Why was this important? When did you learn it? What lesson do you wish you had learned sooner?

Were you ever underestimated because you're a woman? How did you cope with that? Did raising a family interfere with your career?

If you could (or had to) go back to school, what would you study?

Are you better at math or spelling? Has that served you well? Would you have preferred that it be the other way around?

Tell me about an embarrassing moment you had in school. What about an embarrassing moment at work? And just in general? Would you still be embarrassed if it happened today? What did you learn from each of these events?

I'd like you to share some wisdom about friendship. What do you consider the most important quality in a friend? Do you think it's important to have close friends outside the family? Why? Do you wish you had spent more time with friends or stayed in better touch over the years?

What's a recent life lesson that you've learned? Tell me the circumstances. Do you wish you'd learned it sooner?

What do you see as your greatest accomplishment? Was this difficult to accomplish? Why does it make you proud?

CHAPTER 8

Edits and Revisions: Things She'd Change and Things She Wouldn't

Everyone has something they'd do differently, but, sadly, there isn't always the opportunity for a do-over. No one goes through life without regrets, nor should they. It's how you handle those regrets that's important.

Knowing what someone might have done differently in life—or what they wouldn't have—can offer insights into their temperament, their judgment, and what they value. The questions in this chapter allow these kinds of insights into your mom. Some questions are about regrets, others about potential do-overs. Do her regrets involve things she did or didn't do? Is there someone she should apologize to? How might she handle a difficult situation differently today if she could?

Still other questions involve things that might have been different. Where, besides home, would she choose to live? What technological advancement might we all be better off without?

As you learn what Mom would and would not change about her life, think about how you live your own life and the regrets you don't want to have someday.

Is there an invitation—maybe to a party, a date, or just for coffee—that you declined and regret? Why did you decline? Why do you regret it?

If you could pick a day to relive, what would it be? Is that because you'd want to enjoy it all over again? If you'd want it to turn out differently, what would you do to change the outcome?

If you could live somewhere else, where would it be?

What is your favorite place you've ever visited? Have you been back? If you could travel anywhere tomorrow, where would you go? What was the worst vacation you went on?

Do any silly little regrets keep you up at night? What are they? When you look back over your life so far, do you see a common thread in regrets? Do they involve things you did, or things you didn't do?

What has been the most rewarding thing in your life?

Is there someone you should apologize to but haven't? Why?

What's the hardest thing you've ever had to do? Would you handle it differently today? In what way?

If you could pick just one thing to do differently or turn out differently in your life, what would it be?

Are you better at keeping secrets or telling them? Did you ever share someone's secret that you later regretted? Tell me about it.

What's the worst betrayal you've experienced? Have you forgiven the person who betrayed you?

Of all the technological advancements you've seen in your lifetime, from microwaves to cell phones to social media, which do you consider most helpful? Which do you think have been harmful?

Is there anything about your life that you never would have expected?

CHAPTER 9

Turning the Page: Looking Back, Looking Ahead, and Final Thoughts

We've arrived at the final chapter, where you'll explore, among other things, the last part of Mom's story. Death is an inevitable part of life, but conversations about it aren't. Yet knowing how Mom feels about death and dying may make it easier for both of you when that time eventually, inevitably comes. Does she believe in an afterlife? Is she afraid to die?

Don't worry—not all questions in this chapter are that heavy. Some give Mom the opportunity to reflect on memorable moments, like the time someone gave her a really nice compliment. Or the chance to remember and talk about someone who's had a big impact on her life.

You've probably heard it said that one should never discuss politics or religion in polite company. And while we're sure that Mom raised you with proper manners, we are going there. How have her views on politics and religion or spirituality evolved over time? You're about to find out.

This chapter offers up an assortment of existential questions about both life and death, and also lets Mom ask a question or two of her own. So go ahead, turn the page and dig in.

How do you want to be remembered? Is that how you think you'll be remembered? Have you spent much time thinking about your legacy?

Mom, is there something about me that you've always wondered about or would like to ask me now? (You should answer the question and record it, as well as Mom's reaction.)

What are your views on religion and/or spirituality? How have these views changed since you were younger?

How have your political views evolved over the years? Who was the first president you voted for? What historically significant events have you experienced, and how did they impact you?

Can you tell me about a time in your life when you struggled to accept something? How long did it take you to accept the situation? What did this teach you about acceptance going forward?

Has anyone ever been kind to you in a way that you never forgot?

What's the nicest compliment you ever received? Why were you touched by it?

What person has been most influential in your life? Tell me more
about this person. In what specific ways did he or she influence you?

If you could plan your last meal, what would it be?

What do you believe happens after you die? Do you think about your death? Are you afraid to die?

If you could learn exactly when and how you were going to die,
would you want to know? Why or why not?

What did you think of going through these questions?

Is there anything I didn't ask you that I should have?

AFTERWORD

The Story of Mom is done but not over. We hope you'll refer to this keepsake again and again, to remember Mom and relive these memories. We've provided this space for additional thoughts. Maybe one or both of you would like to reflect on what it was like to do the kind of contemplation that many of these questions require. If a significant detail or anecdote occurs to you later, it will have a home here. Fill this space whenever you choose—soon after finishing the journey, or perhaps after Mom passes.

NOTES

Photo
ALBUM

Use the next few pages to affix some of your favorite photos. Be sure to include at least one photograph from all ages and stages of Mom's life: a baby picture, photos of her as a young child and teenager, school photos, a graduation photo, or wedding photo. Include pictures from holidays and seminal family events: a baptism, bat mitzvah, adoption ceremony, quinceañera, breaking the fast on Eid al-Fitr, or celebrating Christmas or Diwali. You might even include a treasured recipe. Don't forget to select a few photos that capture the essence of Mom, or that simply make you smile.